Random Chemicals and Snotty Love Poems
By Pupola

This collection of poems is dedicated to family and friends.

RUBI ENTERPRISE

RUBI ENTERPRISE

[Books Supplier, Publishers & Subscription Agents since 1995]

P.O. Box 5247 (New Market)
Dhaka-1205, Bangladesh.
Tel.: 88-02-9662070, 01715010058
Fax: 88-02-8624571
Email: enquire@rubibook.com
www.rubibook.com

First Published: May, 2011

ISBN: 978-984-33-2493-1

Cover design by Mohammad Zakir Hossain

Illustration by Mohammad Zakir Hossain and Sharmin Zaman

Published by Rokib Uddin Ahmed, Rubi Enterprise, Dhaka. Computer design and produced by Borhan Kabir Apu and Printed at Mother Printers, 8, 10, Nilkhet Babupura, Dhaka-1205, Bangladesh

Forword by Pupola's Father

I am the one who gave her the nickname Pupola, hoping it to be unique. When Pupola was born, I was teaching in the Civil Engineering Department of BUET as a Lecturer. I left for USA in the early 1980's for higher studies. Pupola and her mother Shayla S. Ali (Ankhi), a Civil Engineer herself and my classmate from the Civil Engineering Department of BUET, joined me in the USA a year later.

I suppose like any normal father, I didn't notice when Pupola grew up, let alone when she started writing. Pupola's writing ability first caught my attention when she emailed her mother and me the story "Cover Your Ears". Both her mother and I were impressed by the fluidity of her writing style and the way she immerged herself into the hearts of the characters of her story to fish out simplest honest truths:

> *The girl who was incredibly foolish to have faith that her universe was endless and love was eternal had died in some other unforgotten place. She couldn't do it anymore and joined Quinn in giving up. They both had fought too long with themselves, both were too exhausted. It wasn't romantic. ………. There are no seals for eternity just simple honesty.*

I was later exposed to some of her poems, especially when she expressed an interest in including one or two of her poems in the local Bengali magazine "Seattle-er Chithi". This magazine is published occasionally by the ethnic Bengalis who live in Greater Seattle area in the State of Washington. The poem "Heart Under Glass" was included in the third issue of Seattle-er Chithi.

This poem made me feel the grace of a dance in which the longings for love take wing and the despairs of love keep crushing down: "But the moon gets covered by clouds. The music ends and his existence disappears." I sensed the swing of waltz in the rhythm of the poem:

They twirl and spin around
The dusty universe upon
Destiny's broken glass
For the circling stars waltz
To a well known thought

Through her poems, Pupola travels from the pleasures of momentary bliss to the darkness of heart, from the beauty of love to the despair of broken promises, from the cruelties of harsh realities to the solace of fairy tales. I hope the poems touch some of you. I hope you discover deep personal connections with the genuine feelings youthfully captured in these poems.

Even though Pupola speaks broken Bengali and mostly understands our conversations in Bengali, there is no question English is her first language. Pupola is a first-generation Bangladeshi-American who is proud of her Bengali roots and always feels enriched by her culture. Pupola wrote the poems in this collection mostly during her undergraduate years and a handful as a high school student.

I have a hunch there are many Bangladeshis, young and old, at home and abroad, who wonder about the mental makeup of first-generation Bangladeshi-Americans. Here I present Pupola's original collection of poems to Bangladeshi young adults and grown-ups in the hope of satisfying some of that curiosity about first-generation Bangladeshi-Americans like Pupola.

Dr. Ashraf Ali, D.Sc., MBA
Pupola's Father
Seattle, Washington, USA
Former Lecturer, Civil Engineering Department
BUET, Dhaka

Table of Contents

SNOTTY LOVE POEMS

POSTSCRIPT

Random Chemicals

A Lover's Farewell

I must commit adultery, love
Please forgive me, my dear heart

I need to shut the book
And learn from the hairy beast
To master proper grammar
Perfect my spelling and
Correct punctuation

I will seduce the hairy bastard
When it blindly accepts me
In its bed, I will hack
Of itz head

Hopefully, I can return to
Your embrace by then
So please forgive me while
I learn to
Commit the ultimate sin
Now, I must say good-bye,
Dear heart

Farewell, my love

A Secret Beating

I rip apart your rib cage
To get to the heart
With my bare claws
Liking how the
Blood drips down
My pink-polished nails,
As I feel the warm
Chunkiness inside
So, this is who you are
While an autumn leaf
Brushes past my face
And then I toss
Your squished heart
Back to you

A Secret to a Woman's Heart

Gallons and gallons
of tofu (soft not fried)
is the way to my heart
And sits so nicely
in the bottom of
my tummy for hours
and hours and
hours....

Again

* Something lost
  Something gone
  Can someone please
  Help me?

♦ Okay, that's something
  I can do
  Was it inside a
  Thin cardboard box,
  Covered with paper stars?
  A favorite old book,
  A necklace, or
  Fiery red ring?
  Could it be a goose
  That can lay golden eggs?
  An old baby toy?
  Goat?
  Cell phone?

Beeper?
Keys to your house
And car?
Is it a missing
Thought, memories,
Or dreams?
A certain belief?
An emotion, possibly?

* Never mind, I found it

♦ You'll probably misplace
  It several times
  More…….

* True, but there's always
  Hope to discover it
  Again

All there is

I heard the flowers and grass weed grow
The rain dripped down from a black-stained sky
Tiny water droplets
nourished the child napping within the soil
Moonlight shadows played away, and
the fragrance of petals swirled around in the air

I stood still in the garden of my making,
as the wind always whispered in my ear,
"You are not alone"

Another Walk

gone is this moment known as forever
flown towards the stars
caught a ship going southwest
towards another quest to eternity
Endlessness is quite never that
near or far away inside the heart
Away, away, away to the
Imagined Unknown
To some place unexplored
To a new beginning
To the same old endings

A Beautiful, Wild, Dark Thing

I wanted to find the truth
before I left and found
myself looking again

The only thing I found was
far more possibilities
existing faraway
in separate spheres

I felt myself groping
around in the dark,
but I was more lost
in my own bubble

Then I looked around
to see a whole new
world inside this
rainbow bubble
It was for me alone
to create

I stood up and gave birth

to new possibilities within
my own sphere and slowly
in time to understand
of the other bubbles

Some were in my reach or
just city spheres and some
were million miles way
beyond my comprehension and
distance

But at the end, I don't mind
if I ever find the only truth,
for I have learned of many
more and with my limited mind
seen the brilliance of those
so faraway

If I stay true all the way
that is the only truth
I need to know amongst so
many other ones

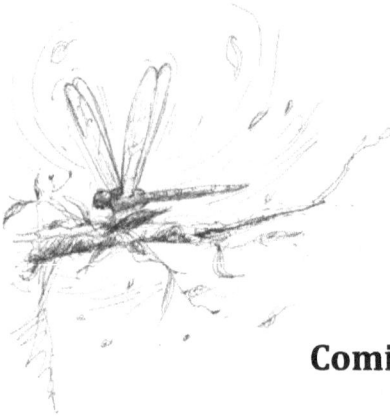

Comings and Goings

The wind rustles
A little heart has flown away
The moment of freedom
Seems so far away
Why is life full of
Illusions inside the
big Head?
Chasing phantoms into
The winds
Ghosts, nothing more
Than passing flights
On broken wings
The breeze comes again,
And this dragonfly
Will find the air
Currents that were
Always there
From the start

Creation

The mother finishes shaping the clay ball and lifts
It off from her spinning wheel
Placing it into the fire to harden
When done, a perfect Earth sphere is formed
Handing over to the father, he blows his breath across it
Water and clouds are formed
He gives it to the brother and sister
It slips from their hands
Cracks has appeared
They pick it up and kiss the
Cracks away and
Life begins

Cruel Ignorance

The backyard trees
Sway, and the breeze
Gently patted my head
While I watered my
Vibrant, wild red roses
Oh, what suburbia bliss
Poverty and corruption
Exist only in fairy tales
While the starved
Naked child with its
Dirty out-stretched hand
Asks what happened to
Human kindness

Oh, I spotted a
Fantastic rainbow in
The sky
Today is truly a
Beautiful day

Cruelty of Age-Old Big Mouths

A thousand colors fell on me,
but it was simply the rainfall
The water drops just splattered
on my hair
No longer turning into
Tiny diamonds sparkling in
the light

As my arms, hands, fingers
grew longer, I learned I
could no longer grab
rainbows and pinch the sky,
and the clouds flew higher
with the blue sky

My mouth and tongue became
brittle and dry cuz reason
and logic burned my mind
away so there's no
more need to say
from the heart

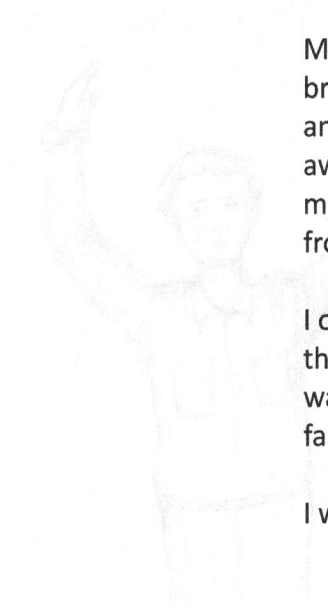

I only now can distort
the world into a
wavy blur with my
fallen tears

I wonder why?

Daily Routines

Let the stars fall from the sky
Shattering against the night winds
Tumbling down upon me, opening
My sins and regrets as the red hurt
Pour down my skin to the
Ground below, absorbing the old blood
To give birth to something new

A sprinkle of snowflakes kisses away
The wounds, and the sunrise will
Dry me off for a start of
Another day

Darkness in The Light

In the darkness, tears are
Not so easy to see
The merciful moonlight cannot
Help make the teary water
Shine in its
Thick
Blackness

Can't sunlight illuminate the
Loneliness and despair in
The happy girl's eyes,
Unseen in the night?

Yet, the kind light that brightens
Frowns to smiles and
                  naive
Happy sighs in the morning minutes
To known cries in the afternoon hours,
Casts l   o   n   g
Shadows, where her
Sadness hides

Disappearing.............

No more sayings about the cold or blessed world
I'd rather lay back and see the snow, white
mountains, fly across the blue sky.

Tired of all the secrets our government
hides behind his back;
I want to see a waterfall bang its self-tormented
aggression on the pool of waters below.

Don't want to follow preachers who lead us to
our doom instead of salvation.

Watch the golden rules from the human heart
fade away in the dying sunset.

What's happening to simple tranquility?

Dwelling

There is no more
Sound to laugh
The tears dried
Up so long ago

To live in the
Present is   futile
The possibilities do
Not exist for
Tomorrow

A past is
All left
To know

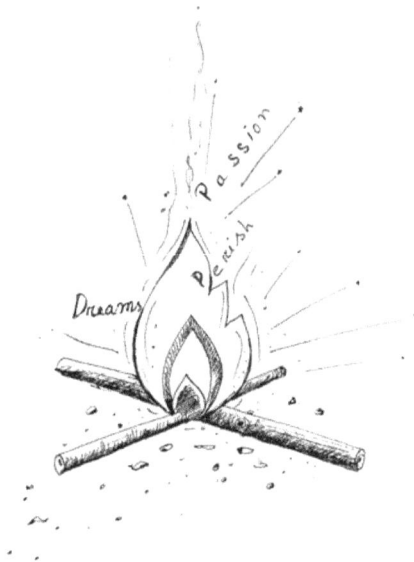

Explosion

Dreams becoming words
Words to crumbling ashes
This insanity leading to unexplored plains
Depths so strange,
pointing towards heights of
passion
Exploding in fireworks
In madness I find what it means to live
In this madness my existence will perish

Fairy Tale Worlds

I might say, "Your poems are better
Than mine", and you might say,
"No, you're the true poet not I"
We could sit here and debate, analyze,
Philosophize all through the night
And this could go on forever with
No winner or loser, but what
Remains true, you and I only want
To share our fairy tale worlds with
The rest of the world

You, me, and others alike will continue
This debate, until one day one person's
Fairy tale world is what
We're all wishing for

Yet, I may turn to you today and
Still say, "Poetry is far richer
In your blood and heart than mine",
But I made an old promise long ago
Not to be afraid to tell
My dreams with the people
Of this world

Fanatic

Why is the sky smurf blue?
Why is the grass jello green?
And why such familiar things?
"Cuz man, I only write
honey-words just for you"

Forever Wrong

Should I blind your seeing eyes
          with beautiful illusions?
Would it be better to paint appealing
               images across your canvas
                    with brushstrokes
                         of our pens?

Do you need us to solve life's problems,
          or remind you of lost
                         yesterdays?
Should we astound you with our
          own philosophy?
How about if we charm you with
          words that make no sense?

What will it take to make you listen
          and remember us?
Just tell us and we'll do, even
          if it's only a minute of
                    your time
Is that what we need to ask?

What are the secret ingredients
          to be known because
               that turns the key
                    to live for
                         eternity.

Freedom

Sour to Sweet=ness
Honey drips Into stars
i Dance joyfully
Beneath Them

Happy Burping Memories
(because nothing could be finer)

I want to remember you
Just now...
Like now...
Right now...

You have moved on with me
You have stayed behind with me,
But the moment has come
For you to leave
Not later...
Nor ever...

Calm your worries and fears,
I honestly can say I'll be dandy
Though, I occasionally
Will bury my head in
Heavenly and hellish fantasies

You guided me to the

Door, and I found
The strength to turn the
Knob
Opening up to new dimensions
The greatest mystery of
All:---> the human self

Thank you, my friend, for
Our journey together has
Come to an end
While you begin anew,
I shall venture on

I know
We will be together again
Like now...
Just now...
Right now...

Beyond Honesty

It's warmer than the
sweet-candy smile
Much more fancier than
the black Mercedes
That just passed by or
the shiny copper
Penny, found on the dusty
floor.

It's the morning sun spilling
honey light on the day
The sparkling stars sighing
over the blue and
White swirls of Earth
a violet rose opening
Its eyes to the new world
in first bloom
The feeling of immorality
when you believe to
Have found your
one and only

It's still here, at yesterday, and today
maybe even longer

Just take a look around

Scattered Fragrance

Oh lovely star,
how you fell from the sky
and blossomed into
the flower of night
In the forest of strange,
you grew ever brighter
Shining louder before
because your heart is full
of cosmic light

How you fell from the sky,
guided by the moon's
Earth shadows below
But only here, all life dies
Laughter fades and reborn in
the midnight black stream
Where your fiery petals
drift next, only
the evening-time cricket
can hop and hum about

Let's Pretend to Dance

I can't ever learn these new steps,
so letz pretend we can dance
Won't you join me in this charade?

We can hide in the superficial
swirl and twirl because thatz
the new fad and the rest won't
bother to find out about our flaws

So let the hellish fire burn our soul to
a crisp while we bump and spin away to
our delusions

Man's Environment

Hearing noises from a creature
Walking   back
And
                              forth
On a jungle island
Hand upon the forehead, hoping
With gentle pressure on
The inner brain to alert
Druggish senses

This mysterious creature makes
White scratches on black
Palm tree leaves with her paws,
Doing what nature calls

The creature's noises dance
Meaninglessly in the
Jungle air
Human eyeballs held in an
Unmoving gaze

Resistance finally falls, giving
Up to nature's power

Gradually being pulled into
Darkness, shaped in
A colorless sphere

What? The creature's sounds,
Make sense! She stares
Straight to the background
Her human gray eyes
Causes fear to push
Nature away

The dense tress dissolve
Into wooden desks
Island sand becomes flat
Carpet

Two violet eyes are now
Wide and open as
The sunny skies,
"Huh? What was the
Question?" the little
Girl asks.

Sea B=lue

The water seems so cold and cruel
Funny, that something like H2O could
Be so foreign for a sweet mermaid like you
Why did something you love so much turn
Against you, filling your bright blue eyes
With confusion and loss?
Who'd thought that an ocean could
Almost drown its own mermaid?
So now you sit there on the rocky beach,
Breathing in oxygen such an unusual air
For you
But your mermaid friends have suffered and felt
The same way too
We'll join you on that rocky shore, determined
To stay in human form as long as it takes
We'll tell you ocean tales of the clam who fought
To keep its pearl from the starfish till the very end
And the salmon fishes who go against the
Raging rivers to fulfill their only one dream
And finally die in peace
We have sworn in our ocean made hearts to remain
By your side until the day you can say good-bye
To your toes and feet and found the courage
That always there on the sandy floors inside
Your ocean made heart
We'll jump in the water together, turning our legs
Into fishy scales, and your mermaid friends will
Sing sweeter than the sirens when we watch you
Accomplish your dreams beneath the sun lit waves
Then you'll remember how wonderful it was
To swim in the ocean blue

My Death Wish

I sat on the edge
of the crescent moon today
and watched the sun peak
behind the earth
in a sunrise

From here, I could
glimpse at
Saturn's rings
Gaze at a meteorite
committing suicide on Mars
while Pluto
desperately wanted to be
part of something more

How I wish my soul
could run freely
throughout the universe
Embracing all the
stars with my heart

My Moon Phases

Some days and nights,
a river of words flows bubbly
from my mouth

Other times when
the digital TV is loud,

I feel...
I speak...
My posture...
Elegantly stiff....
I burp

In the left over mili-seconds,

I would randomly rather

     be ver-
        bally
      pla-
        y-f-u-l-l

Altogether at the end of it all,
      I am left with a smile ^.^

My Patient Friend and Lover

As you walk through life,
your art will trail beside you
As you change the color of your shades,
Your heart will sing it through art

And if you will, or perhaps
by its own accord, your art
may embrace in its warm arms

If you one day choose to love
Your art fully with your heart,
It will become your salvation and
hell
One instant in lover's bliss, later
your heart's torment

So I alone decided this fate, my art
became my torture and
soul mate

Floating Seaweed

Immersed in the waves
Pulled by the ceaseless
moon tides
Loosened from the bottom
of the world
Washed up ashore,
a water fairy's misplaced
pearl of coral reef

Salty ocean air tarnished
the white diamond
of the sea to careless
waterweed; clinging to
the side of
broken amber stones
Once holding endless
wishes from the
silver-blue currents,
now a snack
for sunlit beach insects

Within The Night

Listening quietly as the moon climbs into the sky
Softly smiling behind the reflection of the face in a glass window
Waiting and seeking each star that
Appears above this house where
A new family now lives

Black-silver strands wrapped, unwrapped, wrapped
In a continuous cycle around a finger,
Thinking away to the past where the stars, moon of today and
Tomorrows still come to visit the night, shining silver-white;
Inky shadows gently swaying to the colorless winds

Lullabies of sleep can be soundlessly heard, turning over to
Face shadowed leaves painted
On the walls by the moon
Peace in dreams is finally found after closing sleepy eyes

Nourishment

Dreams plastered
across the sand
Set free by the skip and
a hop of a child's feet
Blood tears to
crystal clear
What's more beautiful
than seeing a
butterfly's broken
wing heal?
Where thoughts
become spoken
words & your loved
ones finally know

One Golden Locket

So many dreams
breeze past by me
Feeling the coolness and
freshness they bring,
blowing my groomed hair
all over the place

Sigh....how so many
dreams tonight
Some shiny-bursting new
mingled with cherished,
faded-old gold

And the memories drift down
like snowflakes
Each intricate and mysterious
designs
Let rushing out by the

secretive heart

Hmm....bittersweet tingles
as the snowflakes melt in
my unkempt, windy hair
and skin

If only I could carry this
all in one golden locket
around my neck, resting
against my beating heart

For all that is given,
a happy tear frozen
like a snowflake and
carried away by the
dreamy breeze to the
twinkling stars

Outside and Inside for This

As the days slip away from my open palms, I want to
capture what I do not know yet before the last day is
swept into the past and the future no longer holds
my dinner reservations

Let me stay here and live in soft pastels
and soar upon a butterfly's rainbow wings
Where I can pluck flower stars from their
lily pads floating in content on the night sky
The stars I gathered in my hands glisten from
water droplets now soaking my skin
Wind pieces of black silk dry off the night
from my hands
I silently smile and earth below sings
Resting my head gently upon the butterfly's back, we
fly towards my friend the moon and I shall give her
star flowers to smell

But the warm light diffuses in the midnight blue ocean
and I must always awake to this sun shining from above
With my palms open another day has become yesterday
Still searching and wondering where the beginning is and
when my last day is no longer mine to hold at least
let me stay forever here, knowing this

Perceived Distances

I sat on this little hill
and my mother on
another, 30 feet away
Yellow and blue roses caught
my mother's eyes since
she was a plant freak
you know

I moved my head sideways,
left-right, up-down
sideways
up-right
up-left
left-down
right-down

She hollered loudly what
I was doing and I yelled

back I am a bird in a tree

Then her voice traveled
through 30 feet of
dandelions between our hills
to say, you are a human
being

I walked over and sat with
my mom on her hill
Together we moved and turned
our heads in all sorts of
delightful ways

She later replied,
"I see..Itz quite fun
turning your head like
a bird in a tree"

Pure Madness

Carey, barey, mary, gary

zerl, derl, terl, sweet old yerl

grr, mrr, .06, 7, and x

Can't comprehend? Then take

my hand

We'll fox trot-waltz to la-de-la-bah land

Reality or Myth?

Who was this person named
William Shakespeare
That captured the hearts of
People in his time
And the beyond?

Some say he never existed
But was a myth humanity
Created for their own
Wishful thinking
Maybe Shakespeare is
Not a man
What if an alien writer
From Saturn?

Please excuse my silly
Thoughts..........

Perhaps, W. Shakespeare
Is merely a good
Disguise for a woman playing
With a grand name

Myth or real, Shakespe.'s
Words always seem to
Hold true in one particular poem:
                    (same?)
 "Even if a poet sits upon
Holy clouds or burn in the
Fires of hell their poems
Will live in the old and
The new"

Or is that only a reality
To a young and poet's
Fancy?

Reliving Higher Conscious

Bring back the pain, the screams
    Into the night, and
The sore red skin from many salty tears
    It was then the memories
Of her were fresh inside my mind

She was the revolution that
    Caused my evolution

Reopen the scars of long ago,
    Let my heart bleed red
And warm down my chest instead
    Cold and blue inside

With her, I could see beyond the simple
    Blue, cloudy skies,
But her revolution shortly ended
    So here, nature decided
To end my evolution while the
    Sands of our broken
Hour glass, slowly devours
      My brain
          Away
Please,
Don't let
Me forget
     My revolution...........

Return to Prose: Retired Spurs of the Moment

-Talking fruits rotted out of long since
years became popular vintage beer
-"A classic!" the beer bellies belch in
unison

-The neon blue aliens have finally tired
of playing limbo
-They jumped into their rusty spaceships,
sputtering past stars and look forward to
greasy pizza; popular old reruns of
Brady Bunch back home

-Ken or Barbie already were sent to the
Emergency Room for 3 to 6 degrees burns
-"Not to forget plastic head decapitations, leg,
or arm detachments," scurrying Meds remind

-All the freaks and loons have gotten married
with 3-2 children
-"Along the side a respectable career," friendly
neighbors vouch

-The animal humans devolved and captured
by many famous zoos
-"An exotic collection," the pooper scoopers say

85 to 90 years: goddess Feela has nothing more
to play
Wait! Ah...........Oh! I know!

*Pearly, porcelain dentures from hell and
beeping pace maker communicating to a
dead, drunken Socrates---spouting out
ancient Japanese

Revival

I want to kiss a star
With my bare lips
Marvel at its internal shine
While holding it in my hands
And not believing the stars are out
Of my reach in the sky and
Not bigger than the palms of my hand

I want to throw out my arms open wide,
High into the air;
Embracing the sunlight, the winds, trees,
All living beings, as much as I can hold and
Release my heart into waves of flood, drowning
Everything with hope and love;
To share the rush of life that flows
Uncontrollably throughout my soul

I want to run with no care but in pure joy
And catch a millions of people's hands
With each of my two hands and not
Deduct I can only hold two
I want to see your soul from the first
Impressions, away from the usual social
Formalities
So, tell me of your dreams, tell me of your
Joys, your fears, and I will show you mine

I know you are hiding behind tree shadows,
Overwhelmed by their domination
Step out of the shadows,
So that the stars can finally say hello
To you
It's okay I need to too
Let's stand there together, so the moonlight
And starlight can heal our old scars
And fresh wounds
Then we will turn to each other and smile as
The tears run freely down our faces at our
Return to ourselves
Then we will be free....to love all

Majestic Beauty

One inch by twelve inch
Polished wood
Each side with numbered marks
Across the ruler like
Black and white piano keys
Is a work of artistic beauty

Conceived in the depths
Of human inspiration
No more arms or legs to measure
Once born to physical form
A simple idea, its cause
Magnificent

The ruler, a rectangular paint brush
The paint different
Measurement and lines
Creating, connecting lines for shape

Aiding the human to develop
Artistic, geometric objects
Holding physical beauty of
Emotions which
The ruler does not possess,
But the unique splendors of
The thinking mind.

Shades and Contrasts

Standing in broken fields we have
Fallen down to the ground far
Too many times to tell
Lost in two worlds blur into one
Half black, half white issues
Must break to find all the shades
And grays we keep inside the heart
Our missing colors should swirl and twirl
For we are not just one color or one song
Ecstasy resides in the release of our
Multi-colored dreams and contradictory
Thoughts that clash against the world
Then forever it is added to
The great dance creating all
Kinds of hues in similarity and
Contrasts to the human spectrum

Shameless Winds

The winds ruthlessly shake and break droopy   R
Branches;
Their dead dreams scattered below
People come to marvel in
Leaves no longer green   I
The circular light high,   S
A tree will   E

Small Things

Hold me soft
But hold me close
Please don't whisper
Any words

Just let me hear
The beating of
Your heart to
Soothe my troubled
Soul

Caught in a Magical Spell

I love this enchantment
Right now, where every word
I'll write won't be
So dry in this clear night
Of silvery stars

All the words I need to
Say comes naturally
With each pen stroke
I create when the
Spell has been cast

It's good to know and
Feel that the magic of
Poetry is still being
Pumped out by
My heart, circulating
Through the blood
In my veins

Still

S   A   S

          T   R

                    (up above myself)

                         me the moon
                    a   g
                    r   o
                    o   i
                       n d   g n

childhood faraway   death still faraway
                    in the middle
                         am I

smearD   tsniagA   eimeT

                                                  or any

I   o   c   o   n   s

                    a   i   t

The Crush

Beating....
My heart thumping
My teeth pinching my lips
My eyes trace his every footstep
I sigh.

The Disgusting Truth

You make me sick!
Your existence
Shares the same level with fish gutz!

I am ashamed to call myself
a human being when I look
at your rotting form

Where's your heart?
Where's your humanity?
I can't even see the
shine of your soul within your eyes

I only can see the slime oozing
out of your blind eyes
How can you call this living?
You are already dead to my eyes

Come on! Get off it, Man!
Show your anger!

Bite and scratch
away to your heart
Light the candle to bring
your soul out of the dark and
discover the passion to find
your own truth
Then you will know what it means to be alive;
to be a full breathing-living human being

But you are trapped as a doll I see
Forever following society's damnation
in sensible convention
Fine, here! Enjoy this half baked
cookie that you wish to swallow

You don't deserve any of my sympathy or pity
Just disappear like the empty lie you are
along with the blind stupid goats that
dare call themselves part of humanity

This Is What I Understand

I am taken by the traveling rainbow,
Flying down the gray sky on
A sunless day
Seeing the shine in people's eyes;
Talking of their dreams and passions
Makes me we want to smile as
We pass each other by

The wooden pipe wordless tune carries
Me away to another far of life when
I close my eyes
Shadows dancing wildly, so freely with
An exotic way around a flame with the
Winds of the sky hold the allure of
Ancient secrets to be known

The sparkles and twinkles of stars
Are just waiting to for someone to
Hear their tales like the silver
Shimmers of the seas, you know

And then my heart bursts with song
When I feel these things

Trapped Within This Beauty

I'm encaged in this
gorgeous hell
Where no words can
capture its entirety, but
I will try to describe
as I go along

The universe is a rose
garden crafted in
stain glass and
the light shining
through is an ever
big mystery

I cannot help but
stand in awe
of this, the enormity,
the magnificence
of it all

I'm breathless, stunned
to blindness, the words
can barely be found
To find the explanation,
to give meaning
burns in desperation
in my soul

I will forever search
Give up my sanity
and status of respectability
during the process
For I shall be staring
at the red glass universe
Till the last blood flow ceases
in my veins until my eyes lose
its spark of hope
I feel; I know this is the truth
of my very existence

Wavering Dreams

The sunlight dims
The song has ended
The birds stop to listen
to the silence the girl
brings

Stepping outside,
the world quiets to
a girl's sad thoughts
Yet the winds blow her
fragrant hair across
her face
The branches sway in a
rainbow arc while the
leaves fan in the breeze

She smiles as memories
of climbing trees
turns into a happy
shine, sparkling
in her eyes, and
her heart becomes free

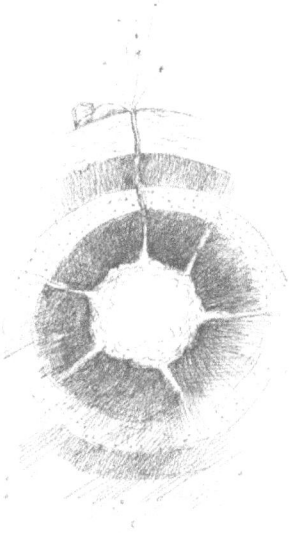

When the End is here

Hiding, hiding away but the truth is
almost here
Hide it again, keep it to yourself
Hide it from thyself until the end is near
and everything will be revealed

Whirlwind

For the world within
For the world without
I exist in all
in memories of
others already be
They can find me
and inside
They are there
as well
For almost autumn leaves
Falling down stardust
Resting peacefully
under a tree if
there any be
To wish for violet petal
ashes set free
if can be in the
milky dew of heavens
Bounded only to the
expanding universe
my scattered-torn soul

An escapement from
this current state

Whispers of Destiny

La, La, La, La, La, La
Hmm, Hm, Hm, Hm, Hm

The rage of injustice is called forth by war horns
The passion set a blaze has burned out the harmless
stars reflected in your eyes

Let's use all of our energy till the very end
but the path you follow only you can choose

Courage has blinded your heart to your first belief of a
righteous way
Pull out your sword and point it to your enemy
if you have the strength
Don't be hasty, dropping your golden sword in the middle
of battle when you change your mind

Have no regrets for the mistakes you can now see; the wounds
in your heart will
never fully heal and the memories will always bleed

Let's shine forever as the silver stars
till we can no longer fight destiny
The path we follow will burn forever as a light inside our hearts
But the choices to make are left only for you;
the whispers of destiny

La, La, La, La, La, La
Hmm, Hm, Hm, Hm, Hm

Why?

If..................

Everything is based upon or
A lie to a promise to
Tell others and a false
Possibility for the dreams
Inside the heart forever

The invisible life has lain out
All the wonderful treasures
Before the feet, the only
Rule is to make ones
Dream come true

So why not do that?

Why not go through the
Hardships; use
Potential energy to kinetic energy
And produce wonderful things?
Instead the right times slip
Away, as the
Seconds pass by

What are the mysteries to

Let precious gifts given
To merely rot in
Life's outstretched hands?

Is it the fear to begin the
Fire and only watch
The flame be extinguished
With all efforts burnt
To nothing?

Or is obtaining the romantic
Mind leads to cosmic
Thoughts but with the
Inability to fight
The challenges along the way?
Or is being a coward
An easier life?

We are not the gallant
Conquer of our old dreams,
Possibly......

The question still left unanswered
Just one word
Why?

With Sincerity and Heart

You say, I gave you the
strength to move mountains,
and I am the source of your
inspiration

You even composed a song
on a stringed guitar about me
for goodness sake

You can't help but dream of me
every day, so you say
Constantly you say, I make
you weak in the knees,
but I would rather
give you a pair of silvery
wings to set you free

Yup-Yup-Yup

So, here we go again
Find myself staring
At another kind of wall
Is it another name
For the same thing?

I am sorry Jack
Whoever said eternity
Was everything went
Off the train track
Nothing lasts forever
Even contentment

So, let me bow my
Head & find the
Answer to this riddle
Of mine
Maybe then I can
Smile for awhile

Snotty Love Poems

Faces

I watch your cloudy, blue sky eyes dance,
Gazing around the classroom
But never once in my direction;
You lean your cheek against your hand,
I wonder what show is playing inside your
Theater mind.

I wish you and I were trapped
On a deserted island,
So you'd finally know my name;
Every day, I seek for your face among the
Moving herd of humans in the hallways;
Yet, when I do find you, your face displays
No recognition of my presence, as if I
Was a passing breeze brushing against
Your soft bangs.

I dream of us in a semi-fluid world
While I hide behind other people's
Faces.

Just Before I Go

Please look into my eyes
And finally see the secret
That I well so hide
Take a long hard look
Before you pass me by

I'm trapped inside
This rusted cage that
Once held the color gold
But slowly aged
By acid rain

I lift my head towards
God and pray to let
You simply not walk past
My way before these
Red flames of frustration
Consume me whole

Before I walk out of your life,
Just before I
Reach eternal sleep;
Take one last look into
My black eyes and know
There was a girl who
Once loved you with
Her heart and soul

Unseen Wonders

These feelings beating inside
    My heart would

Drown the islands and seven continents,
    But you were too busy

Observing the seagulls shriek
    In the blue air

If I flooded the universe
    To sweep away

All the stars and wash up in Earth's
    Rocky skies for you,

                Another idle thought is being pondered
                    Inside your head

                Instead of listening to a
                    Starfish convey

                The locations of my buried secrets,
                    Your amusement was

                Found in kicking up
                    Beach sand

                No wonder, in ever realizing this!

Heart Under Glass

The gentleman bows and
She courtesies in the
Lighted ballroom floor
Golden violin strings start
To sing a song; he pulls
Her into a needing embrace
And takes her gentle hand

Slowly stepping side to side
To their own dance,
On broken glass
Music plays in empty air,
Carried away by black breezes
Going past them
They twirl and spin around
The dusty universe upon
Destiny's broken glass
For the circling stars waltz
To a well known thought

Dark ocean waves play
A lovely tune as the tides
Rush against their
Dancing shoes;
A silk sensation of
Midnight blue
Fragmented glass crunched
Under the water

He dips her back
Her arm extends out and
Lightly touches her
Reflected fingers feeling like fluid glass
Lifting her back up to see his
Forgotten face
Their heels contact marble floor
Inside the unlit ballroom

Soft chimes vibrate from
Crushed glass
Beneath their swift feet
Crystal chandeliers hum rainbows
In the presence of moonlight,
Shining from diamond windows
His head tips down for a kiss,
But the moon gets covered
By clouds
The music ends, and his
Existence disappears

Her bare feet seeps crimson
From sharp glass, scattered
All over the shadowed floor
Looking up to stars falling from
The sky, glass snowflakes
Spiraling, flashing silver
Inside her violet eyes
She now closes the blinds
Goodnight

Never There

A fragile smile
thin as sugar
candy sheets
Twinkling hope
in her eyes
Her heart in a canoe
still tied to the
pond's wooden dock
Her dreams full of
swimming fishes
Patiently staying
for the day when
starlight and twilight
would always be hers
He promised her
he would keep
the traveling lady swans
The misty clouds in her
sky could only endure
for so long

As he slept
through the night,
the constant of clouds
became the season of rain
Sugar candy sheets
shattered when her
smile disappeared
Losing the hope
in her wet eyes,
her heart flew away

No power in the
celestial void can
reverse time
like a door key
rusting in his hand
Memories locked inside,
is what we all contain
Easily brushed aside,
as he joined another
lady of the day

Equal Exchange

"Let me sing the troubled words
you cannot speak
I can strum the sound
of your heart beat
on my brittle guitar..."

With teacup in hand,
she remembered
to take a sip
She briefly vanished to a
different melodious world
How did the guitar singer know
in the packed Friday-night cafe?
Her tune of love gone astray
Why ever journey back when
the tale ends the same?

Swaying heads, hands lightly
drumming the stained tabletops
Customers musically lost
The thunder of applause splashed
against the cafe walls, and
the caffeine-energized crowd yelled,
"Encore! Encore!"
She mischievously smirked,
it was her brother's turn to
play about his romantic flare
on his old wooden guitar

What Goes In Must Come Out

Her older sister came
To visit
She brought tales with
Her from the east, south,
West, and north

The younger sister's
Children & her husband
'Oooed' & 'awed' over
That adventure or
Funny predicaments of
The older sister's
Worldwide journey

The eldest sister
Finally left her
Little sister's place
She kissed her nieces
& nephews good-bye
Showered them with
Cool souvenir presents
Of course
To her sis and brother-in-law;
A warm hug,
An "I love you",
And "See you later"

When the older sis
Ran off to another
Destination, the younger
Sister quietly
Sat down on her leather couch
The children went
Outside to play
The husband back
To his study

The little sis looked
Around her house
Pictures of the family
In silver-golden frames and
Hanging decorative pieces
Her laptop on the coffee table
To do work over the weekend
She stared down into
Her royal blue carpet
Her bare feet comfy fine,
But her tear drops
Stained the carpet's lovely
Shine
This was not what she wanted
Not at all
The tears wetted her hands that
Covered her face

She listened to others
They guaranteed this
Was the golden dream
They were wrong,
So wrong

Her older sis was living
The life she wanted
Though her sister's choice
Brought scorn by many
Her older sister
Always brushed them aside,
For she followed
What felt right in
Her heart

The younger sis
Cried again silently
Into her hands
Repeating the same
Phrase over & over again,
"I didn't want this.
It was something else."

Hidden Games

His heart swelled when his
Well buried secret was revealed
The girl blinked in confusion
The boy had hidden his
Feelings for her so well

She politely said no
The boy dreamed before
A different reply
In some other corner,
Another girl did the
Same thing with another boy
The boy gave the same answer

All these rules for all these
Moves to all these secret games
Where did it all come from?
Is it so necessary?
The game of conquest with
Deceptive motives?
You are just playing hide and seek
To those you perceive to love
Don't forget you also play it
With yourself
As well as myself

In My Veins

You invade me like
the slowest of poisons
In my dreams,
your words follow
In this rage,
inside this torment,
you name it sweetness
I stamp out with
my bare hands
and write it as
an inescapable hell

The Lady Ghost that Went Far Into the World

She got tired of the same
Old pattern in 2 hundred
Years or so
The area was reeking
With tourists to see
The haunted lovers' spot

The lady ghost let
Go of dead memories
She jumped back into
The life stream with glee
She had many adventures
On simpler joys of life,
Experienced many other lovers,
Discovered motherhood
A few times,
Found a few scientific
Theories, and formulas too

The lady ghost
Happily continues one
Life after another
Her ex-ghost man
Weeps now for
Her loss in the same spot
The tourists got tired
Of his display and
Ran back to their
Respective homes

All Over

How wonderful there is
Something greater
The existence of life itself
Brought forth the birth of
Families, friends, you,
Me, and the rest of everything
Dear

Isn't it amazing that
Love comes in never ending forms?
Love for the sister, child, parent,
Lovers, cute alligators, the
Universe itself

It's all over my dear
Just not only home-bound near

I don't fear if there is

No possibility of you and me
My oceans of tears already
Filled the universe at
Humanity's broken spirit
My feet and hands are meant
To see and create for all
To Share
Love shouldn't have to beg at
Anyone's feet,
Darling dear
It's freely all over
And right inside here
In your own heart

There is nothing to fear
But everything to feel
It's everywhere, all over,
My dear

Many Great Things

The pattern solved
The cycle ends
And everything begins anew
Through pain, the honest
Truths change us forever
The exact details may
Fade away but the
Memory of those feelings
We never do forget
In agony, the sweetness
Of life is truly felt
And wisdom starts to grow
It's just one of the
Many ways it goes
A new pattern
Spins away while
Another realization
Waits to be learned
That is one of
The ways it
Flows

Life, a Better Story

Don't you know my
Silly-dear friend,
Your life is far richer than
Some unoriginal love story?
An author plays God with their tales
While you can't guarantee how the
Next day will go
Every day, every hour,
Minute, second is an
Opportunity for you to choose
The course of your life
The main character is merely
Controlled by the fate's plotline
Who's to say how friendships
And lovers will go?
Even the repeated routines
Of the day can go astray
You can find joy and heartache
And some lessons along the way
To me, living this mundane reality
Is finer
For life and the self is the
Best mystery story of all

Postscript

A. Bengali translation of one of my poems called "Perceived Distances": My father translated this poem out of sheer curiosity. The original English as well as Bengali translation are presented side by side. - Pupola

Perceived Distances	প্রতীয়মান দূরত্ব
Pupola	পূপলা
I sat on this little hill and my mother on another, 30 feet away Yellow and blue roses caught my mother's eyes since she was a plant freak you know I moved my head sideways, left-right, up-down sideways up-right up-left left-down right-down She hollered loudly what I was doing and I yelled back I am a bird in a tree Then her voice traveled through 30 feet of dandelions between our hills to say, you are a human being	আমি বসেছিলাম ছোট্ট একটি টিলার চূড়ায়, আর আমার মা আরেকটিতে ৩০ ফুট দূরে। হলুদ ও নীল গোলাপ আমার মায়ের দৃষ্টি আকর্ষণ করে, কারণ সে একজন বৃক্ষ বিলাসী, এ তো তোমাদের জানা। আমি আমার মাথা দোলাই এপাশ-ওপাশ বামে-ডানে, উপরে-নীচে এপাশ-ওপাশ উপরে-ডানে উপরে-বামে বামে-নীচে ডানে-নীচে মা চিৎকার করে জানতে চায় আমি কি করছি। আমি সমস্বরে উত্তর করি, আমি গাছে বসা এক পাখি। তার কণ্ঠ তখন আমাদের টিলার মাঝের তিরিশ-ফুট-জোড়া ড্যান্ডিলিয়ন ভেদ করে, বলে- 'তুমি একজন মানুষ'

I walked over and sat with my mom on her hill Together we moved and turned our heads in all sorts of delightful ways She later replied, "I see..Itz quite fun turning your head like a bird in a tree"	আমি হেঁটে গিয়ে আমার মায়ের সাথে বসি তার টিলায় একত্রে আমরা আমাদের মাথা নাড়াই ও দোলাই সব রকম আনন্দমন্ডিত উপায়ে পরে সে উত্তরে বলে, "তাই তো.. গাছে বসা পাখির মতো মাথা এদিক-ওদিক দোলানো তো বেশ মজার"

B. Bengali translation of one of my short stories called "Royal Thorns": My father translated this story back in 2004 to include it in the second issue of a local Bengali Magazine entitled "Seattle-er Chithi", published occasionally by the efforts of Bangladeshis living in Greater Seattle area. Both English and the Bengali versions are given here side by side. - Pupola

Royal Thorns
Pupola

রাজ কন্টক
পূপলা

A splendid old castle stood on a gorgeous mountain. It was the first imperial castle that the land had ever known and since then became an actual small

সুদর্শন পাহাড় চূড়ায় দাঁড়ানো জমকালো পুরাতন এক রাজপ্রাসাদ। এই অঞ্চলের সর্ব প্রথম রাজপ্রাসাদ। রাজপ্রাসাদটি প্রতিষ্ঠার পর থেকে ভূখণ্ডটি একটি ক্ষুদ্রায়তন রাজ্যে পরিণত হয়ে গেল। প্রথম মহান

country. After the passing of the first great just king, the remaining ruling family was thrown into utter turmoil. For you see, a thick dense thorn forest grew around the castle imprisoning the royalty. Getting water was not a problem when a nearby river provided the water in their pipes and food and other necessities were delivered by the villagers. All sorts of people could pass through the thorns with no harm to them going in and out of the castle. It was the royal family who could never set foot out of the castle. The thorn trees viciously attacked the people who had the first royal family blood in them.

This continued on for generations and generations even with marriages mixing other royalty from far off lands. On the country's 100th ruling of the current royal family, King Semi and Queen Fair had 3 children. Two elder boys named Kurane who was the eldest, Aurane was the middle sibling, and

ন্যায়পরায়ন রাজার মৃত্যুর পর রাজ পরিবারের অবশিষ্ট সদস্যরা বিষম এক বিশৃঙ্খলার মধ্যে নিপতিত হলো। ঘটনা কি জানেন, রাজপ্রাসাদের চারপাশ গভীর ঘন কাঁটাবনে ঢেকে গিয়ে রাজপরিবারকে গৃহবন্দী করে ফেললো। পানির সমস্যা ছিল না, কারণ নিকটবর্তী নদী থেকে প্রাসাদের পাইপযোগে পানি সরবরাহ হতো এবং গ্রামবাসীরা খাদ্য ও অন্যান্য অত্যাবশ্যকীয় দ্রব্যাদি এনে দিত। সকল পদের মানুষ কাঁটাবনের ভিতর দিয়ে অনায়াশে প্রাসাদের ভিতরে-বাইরে যাতায়াত করতে পারতো। কিন্তু রাজপরিবারের কেউ প্রাসাদের বাইরে পদার্পন করতে পারতো না। প্রথম রাজপরিবারের রক্তের গন্ধ পেলেই কাঁটাবন নির্মমভাবে আক্রমন করতো।

এমনকি দূর-দূরান্তের রাজ পরিবারে বিয়ের মাধ্যমে রক্ত মিশ্রণের পরেও প্রজন্মের পর প্রজন্ম একই ভাবে চলতে থাকে। বর্তমান রাজপরিবারের একশততম প্রশাসনে রাজা ‘সেমি’ ও রাণী ‘ফেয়ার’ এর তিনটি সন্তান জন্মগ্রহন করলো। বায়োজ্যেষ্ঠ পুত্রটির নাম কুরেইন, মধ্যম পুত্রটির নাম আওরেইন এবং কনিষ্ঠ সন্তান হলো রাজকুমারী খানুরেইন। অতীত কালের রাজ পরিবারের মতো এই রাজ পরিবারও তাদের কন্টক অভিশাপ দূর করণে দৃঢ় প্রতিজ্ঞ ছিল। অতীতে যারা চেষ্টা করেছে তারা সকলেই কন্টকবিদ্ধ হয়ে মৃত্যু বরণ করেছে, কিন্তু কুরেইন ও আওরেইন পূর্ব-

the youngest was the Princess Khanurane. Like the previous ruling families, the family was determined to overcome their thorn curse problem. Those who did try in the past were killed by the thorns but Kurane and Aurane were not going to be scared off from their ancestors' foolish mistakes. They took their families silver and gold swords and marched off past the front entrance gates. The king and queen watched with great anguish their only two sons leave for they did not want any of their children to go. Princess Khanurane kicked the stone wall with her dainty slippers. She may have been given a long name by her father but she was rather short in height.

Princess Khanurane kicked the wall again in frustration. She knew her brothers would never be victorious. They had signed their death contract the minute they stepped out of the safety of the castle surroundings. The queen collapsed into the king's arms when they

পুরুষের নির্বোধ ভুল ও তজ্জনিত দুর্ভাগ্যের ঘটনায় আদৌও ভীত বা বিচলীত নয়। তারা রাজপরিবারের রূপো ও সোনা নির্মিত তরবারী নিয়ে সামনের তোরণ দিয়ে গট গট করে হেঁটে বের হয়ে গেলো। রাজা ও রাণী বেদনার্ত চিত্তে তাদের পুত্র দুটিকে চলে যেতে দেখলো। তারা পুত্রদ্বয়ের যেতে দেবার পক্ষপাতি আদৌও ছিল না।

রাগে দুঃখে রাজকুমারী খানুরেইন তার পরিপাটি স্যান্ডেল দিয়ে পাথরের দেয়ালে পদাঘাত করলো। পিতা তার লম্বা নাম রেখেছে ঠিকই, কিন্তু প্রকৃতপক্ষে সে লম্বায় অনেক খর্বকায়া ছিল। রাজকুমারী খানুরেইন নৈরাশ্যে পুনর্বার দেয়ালে পদাঘাত করলো। সে জান তো তার ভাতৃদ্বয় কখনো জয়যুক্ত হতে পারবে না। রাজপ্রাসাদের নিরাপদ চৌহদ্দির বাইরে পদক্ষেপ করার সাথে সাথে তারা তাদের মৃত্যু-দলিল দস্তখত করে দিয়েছে। প্রিয় পুত্রদ্বয়ের শেষ মরণ চিৎকার কানে ঢোকার সাথে সাথে রানী রাজার বাহুর মধ্যে নিপতিত হলো।

''আমার পুত্র দুইটিকে হারালাম। কেন ওরা আমাদের কথা শুনলো না''? রাজা সেমি তার প্রিয় রাণীকে জড়িয়ে ধরে কাঁদতে লাগলো।

''এর কারণ জানো বাবা, কুরেইন ও আওরেইনের মন লোভে পরিপূর্ণ

heard the fatal cries of their beloved sons.

"I have lost my boys. Why didn't they listen to us?" King Semi wept while embracing his queen love.

"Because father, Kurane and Aurane had greed in their heart. They were not intending to set us free but themselves. You should have heard them last night. All that scheming after ridding of the curse and then doing away with us so they could get the power and gold," Khanurane's eyes were fiery with anger.

"Your grief is causing to say mad things child," King Semi spoke with a teary-face.

"NO! If Kurane and Aurane were noble, they wouldn't be dead now! Only the sacred and the good family members stayed in the castle. The ones with vanity, greed, and evil intentions were slain by the thorn trees. It's all in our royal records, father. No good-hearted ancestors of ours have ever ventured beyond these castle walls,"

ছিল। ওরা আমাদের নয়, বরং নিজেদেরকে মুক্ত করতে চেয়েছিল। তুমি যদি গতকাল রাত্রে ওদের কথা শুনতে। অভিশাপ মোচন শেষে আমাদেরকে অপসারণ করে ক্ষমতা ও সোনা-দানা কব্জা করার জন্য তাদের কত সব পরিকল্পনা"। রাগে রোষে খানুরেইনের চোখ আগুনের মতো জ্বলছিল।

"ভাতৃশোকে কাতর হয়ে তুমি পাগলের মতো অসংলগ্ন কথা বলছো, বাছা", রাজা সেমি অশ্রুভরা চোখে বললো।

"না, তা নয়। কুরেইন ও আওরেইন মহৎ হলে তাদের মৃত্যু কবলিত হতে হতো না। আমাদের পরিবারের পবিত্র ও সৎ সদস্যরাই কেবল প্রাসাদের ভিতর রয়ে গিয়েছে।

অহঙ্কারী, লোভী ও অসদিচ্ছা পরায়ন সদস্যরা কাঁটাবনের হাতে নিহত হয়েছে। এই সকল তথ্য তো আমাদের রাজ-দলিলে স্পষ্টাক্ষরে লিপিবদ্ধ করা আছে, বাবা। আমাদের কোন সদমনা পূর্বপুরুষই এই প্রাসাদ থেকে বের হওয়ার চেষ্টা করেনি", রাজকুমারী খানুরেইন রাগান্বিত হয়ে বলে চললো, "আর সত্য কথা বলতে কি, এসব নিরর্থক কর্মকান্ড দেখে দেখে আমি হয়রান হয়ে গিয়েছি"।

বাবাকে পিছনে ফেলে রাজকুমারী খানুরেইন উলটো গুদাম ঘরের দিকে

Princess Khanurane angrily went on, "And, I am frankly tired of all this nonsense."

Princess Khanurane turned around and fled to the storeroom leaving her father too grief-stricken to say anything else. Princess Khanurane flung open the storeroom door hastily. There were cobwebs and dust as the princess cleared the way with her arms. She found one good old bronze sword stung on the wall. She removed it and headed outside the back way from the kitchen.

The thorn trees immediately recognized the blood of the first family as Khanurane entered the forest. She had no time to use her shiny brown sword. Red vines coiled tightly around her, raising her high into the air.

"I swear by the first great king, I have no greed or evil intent in my heart but to end this curse for my family!" Princess Khanurane yelled loudly with no fear.

"We shall see little one how

দৌড় দিল। বাবা এতটা শোকাচ্ছন্ন ছিলেন যে, তিনি কিছুই বলতে পারলেন না। রাজকুমারী খানুরেইন দ্রুত হাতে গুদাম ঘরের দরজা ঠাস করে খুলে ফেললো। মাকড়সার জাল ও ধূলা দুই হাতে সরিয়ে রাজকুমারী পথ করে নিলো। সে দেয়ালে আটকানো পুরাতন একটি মজবুত পিতলের তরবারী খুঁজে পেল। তরবারি তুলে নিয়ে সে রান্না ঘরের পিছন দিয়ে বাইরের দিকে রওয়ানা হলো।

খানুরেইন প্রবেশ করার সাথে সাথে কাঁটাবন প্রথম রাজপরিবারের রক্ত সনাক্ত করে ফেললো। ঝকঝকে বাদামী রঙের তরবারিটি ব্যবহার করার সুযোগ তার আর হলো না। লাল লতা তাকে শক্ত করে আষ্টেপৃষ্টে জড়িয়ে ধরে শূন্যের মধ্যে তুলে ফেললো।

রাজকুমারী খানুরেইন নিভীক চিত্তে সজোরে বললো, ''আমি প্রথম মহান রাজার নামে শপথ করে বলছি, আমার মধ্যে কোন লোভ বা অসদিচ্ছা নেই। আমি শুধু আমার পরিবারের অভিশাপ মোচন করতে চাই''।

''দেখবো বাছা তোমার হৃদয় সত্যিই কতটা শুদ্ধ'', একটি কণ্ঠ শূন্যের ভিতর থেকে ভেসে আসলো।

''আমার লুকোবার কিছুই নেই'', খানুরেইন নিভীক চিত্তে কাঁটাবনের কাছে পেশ করলো। একটি বিশাল

pure your heart truly is," a voiced bellowed out of nowhere.

"I have nothing to hide!" Khanurane retorted back bravely in the jungle of thorns. A large blood-red thorny vine swiped at her arms and legs. Her cuts bled as the thorns released poison into her blood stream.

Laughter filled the air, "If there is any evil in your heart, you will perish in matter of seconds child!" the voice chuckled mightily.

The poison did nothing to Princess Khanurane and the thorn forest crumbled away. Princess Khanurane landed ungracefully on her butt. In the midst of the breaking thorn forest, the old first king stood tall.

"Princess Khanurane, you have broken our family curse. After all these generations, I have finally found a good fair royal representative to truly rule over this land," the great king revealed.

রক্তলাল কাঁটালতা তার বাহু ও পা আঁচড়িয়ে দিলো। সূচালো কাঁটা তার রক্ত স্রোতের মধ্যে বিষ ঢুকিয়ে দিল। ক্ষত থেকে রক্ত ঝরতে থাকলো।

অট্টহাসি চতুর্দিকের বাতাস আচ্ছন্ন করে ফেললো, ''তোমার মনে অসদিচ্ছার অস্তিত্ব থাকলে তুমি মুহূর্তের মধ্যে ধ্বংস হয়ে যাবে বাছা'', কণ্ঠটি সজোর চাপা হাসি দিলো।

দেখা গেল রাজকুমারী খানুরেইনের উপর বিষের কোনো প্রতিক্রিয়াই হলো না। কাঁটাবন চূর্ণ হয়ে শূন্যে মিলিয়ে গেলো। রাজকুমারী খানুরেইন অনেকটা বেখাপ্পা ভঙ্গীতে নিতম্বের উপর মাটিতে ধপাস করে পড়লো। ভেঙ্গে চূর্ণ হয়ে যাওয়া কাঁটাবনের মাঝখানে বৃদ্ধ প্রথম রাজাকে উচ্চ শীরে দন্ডায়মান দেখা গেলো।

''রাজকুমারী খানুরেইন, তুমি আমাদের পরিবারের অভিশাপ মোচন করেছো। বহু প্রজন্ম অপেক্ষার পর আমি অবশেষে এই রাজ্যে সুষ্ঠুভাবে শাসন করার যোগ্য একজন রাজপ্রতিনিধি পেলাম'', মহান রাজা ব্যক্ত করলেন।

''তুমিই তবে আমাদের পরিবারের ভোগান্তির জন্য দায়ী? শুধু একজন উত্তম শাসক সন্ধানের জন্য? এই বিচারের কি অধিকার তোমার আছে? মহারাজা, রাজ্যের অধিবাসীরা

"You were responsible for our families' sufferings? Just to find a good ruler? What right do you have to judge? Your majesty, villagers of this land picked you to be their king not by your hands alone," Khanurane proclaimed.

"You know your history well, princess but nevertheless our kingdom has a pure hearted ruler now for its people," the first king spoke his final words and disappeared into the wind.

The legendary Queen Khanurane of the 100th ruling broke her old royal families' curse. The fair queen was chosen by her people the same as the first great just king who brought forth the birth of their nation. So as decreed in law in the 100th ruling, the next rulers would be fairly set upon the throne from the free choice of the country's own citizens.

তোমাকে রাজা নির্বাচন করেছিল, তুমি কেবল নিজের প্রচেষ্টায় সম্রাট হও নাই", খানুরেইন ঘোষনা দিলো।

"রাজকুমারী, তুমি তোমার ইতিহাস সম্পর্কে ভালই অবগত আছো মনে হচ্ছে, কিন্তু সে যাই হোক, আমাদের রাজ্য আজ প্রজাকল্যানকারী শুদ্ধ হৃদয়ের একজন শাসক পেয়েছে", প্রথম রাজা তার শেষ শব্দগুলি উচ্চারণ করে বাতাসের মধ্যে মিলিয়ে গেলেন।

কিংবদন্তীর একশততম শাসক রাণী খানুরেইন তার পরিবারের পুরাতন অভিশাপ মোচন করলো। রাজ্যের জন্মদাতা প্রথম মহান বিচারদাতা রাজার মতো ন্যায়পরায়ণ রাণী খানুরেইনও একই ভাবে দেশের প্রজাদের দ্বারা নির্বাচিত হলো। সুতরাং একশততম প্রশাসনে এই মর্মে আইন জারী করা হলো : পরবর্তী প্রশাসকগণ কেবল দেশের জনগণ কর্তৃক মুক্ত নির্বাচনে ন্যায়নিষ্ঠভাবে সিংহাসনে অধিষ্ঠিত হতে পারবে।

C: A short story by Pupola called "Cover Your Ears": The following story was written on Thursday, March 13, 2003.

Cover Your Ears

Sally Bluebell walked into the friendly nonalcoholic bar though smoking was allowed in every nook and cranny of the smelly place. She placed her purse on the counter and comfortably crossed her legs when she sat on the barstool. The smoke was hazy and it matched well to what she was feeling that second. Sally's curly, medium-length hair moved with her head when she turned towards some footsteps that came to her direction. She gave a small nod and smile when she recognized her friend Keith.

"Well, Keith, how are you? Still outing with Tom?" Sally smirked while her friend sat next to the barstool beside her.

Keith gave her a sharp look, "Yes," he said just that.

"That's interesting. No more new notches on your bedpost anymore? A totally new tradition, huh? Too bad, I have a chance to finally beat you," she slightly tilted her head to the side, "Hey, are you still carrying around that cigarette cartoon? Give me one if you would please."

"I have quit, you know but when did you ever start? I thought you weren't that sort," his long fingers pulled out the white cigarette cartoon from his back pant pocket and tossed the pack near Sally's elbow that rested on the bar counter.

"Wrong, buddy-boy," She pulled one cigarette out and asked the bar tender to light it for her, "This would make the second cigarette in my entire life. I just know the consequences of having another and another."

Sally watched the smoke she blew out of her mouth join with the rest of the smoky air in the bar. The cigarette really did match the mood for the setting and the gentle rainfall outside though the sun was strangely out. She knew she was witnessing a revolution with her childhood friend, Keith. It was funnier how calmly she reveled in it. Keith was just Keith from the time she knew him. Now, he was Keith with Tom and most likely for the rest of his life. The reason why was not that bang of a mystery, perhaps just more sorrowful.

"I never thought you would start shopping for a white picket fence in your future. I guess you recently just got it, the moment when your mom slipped away 10 months ago from breast cancer. The things you have left in your life are too precious to waste anymore and that includes me no matter how much I am pissing you off right now. Gee, I feel so blessed. I can get away with anything I say to you," Sally grinned evilly at her reflection in the mirror hanging on the wall behind the counter.

"Enough being a chimney pipe," Keith snatched the nasty cigarette from Sally's mouth and snuffed it out in the greasy crystal ashtray.

"I rest my case," Sally felt a little burst of energy and swiveled her barstool around, "Oh, the mouse finally makes an appearance," Jane the bouncy ball stood a few feet away from her.

"Is it true? Are you really-"

"What? It shouldn't matter to you anymore. You decided that I am worth less than a nickel for your time two years ago and what a reunion. A question not a welcoming hug for a long lost friend," Sally folded her arms against her chest.

Jane's eyes looked downward and for once she did not have the energy to reply back.

"It's all right little woman girl go back to your love pie and your fantastic smurf friends. You know you will always get the happy endings no matter how much you believe that lie," Sally's eyebrow arched up as her earrings dangled a little.

Jane's head popped up in anger, "I wish our paths had never crossed, Sally Bluebell!"

"I am sorry to hear that from your side but I beg to differ. I am glad I met someone who is an immature version of myself. However, you are far cleverer in painting illusions to hide the fact of having a cold stone for a heart. Oh, my date is here. It was nice chatting with you two," Sally took her purse off of the bar counter and left the barstool she sat upon. By the entrance, her date, Quinn, was waiting for her.

"Hello, Sally love. I thought you mentioned you were busy with another for today," Quinn teased.

"Whatever. They can blubber about my absence to my voice box on my cell phone," the two departed from the stinky bar.

"Yup, Sally has changed quite a bit," Keith answered Jane's question in Sally's place, "It's a pity Sally did not meet your requirements for your lovely fantasies you enjoy living in," Keith then left feeling out of the mood to linger any longer.

And in the pretty park with plants covered in water droplets when the rain stopped, Sally looked up into the blue sky. Passion was the only thing that made sense to Sally. It was the only sensible thing that felt like the real truth. Passion was mutual between Quinn and herself nothing more, far more realistic. They were the same always hovering around the borders that threatened to dissolve in their hasty bliss.

It was Quinn who broke the dam first between them and asked for the impossible. She knew she couldn't give in. Her days of giving in were an ancient legacy but she couldn't help feel on the edge in the presence of Quinn who was too much like herself. She kept staring at the clouds moving like slow turtles in the sky till her shoulders vibrated to gradual intensity, and Quinn took her into his comforting arms till her shudders subsided. The girl who was incredibly foolish to have faith that her universe was endless and love was eternal had died in some other unforgotten place. She couldn't do it anymore and joined Quinn in giving up. They both had fought too long with themselves, both were too exhausted. It wasn't romantic. It wasn't a true love song that the radio spewed out. It was raw, needy, and most definitely crude from the start but it felt right since there were no illusions guiding them along the way. There are no seals for eternity just simple honesty.

www.ingramcontent.com/pod-product-compliance
Lightning Source LLC
Chambersburg PA
CBHW070645030426
42337CB00020B/4168